Thinking Out Loud

Nicole Todd

India | USA | UK

Thinking Out Loud © 2024 Nicole Todd

All rights reserved.

No part of this publication may be reproduced, stored in a retrieval system, or transmitted, in any form or by any means, electronic, mechanical, photocopying, recording or otherwise, without the prior written permission of the presenters.

Nicole Todd asserts the moral right to be identified as the author of this work.

Presentation by *BookLeaf Publishing*

Web: www.bookleafpub.com

E-mail: info@bookleafpub.com

ISBN: 9789360949655

First edition 2024

To my mother who has been and still is my anchor. I cannot thank you enough.

To my sister and my partner who supported me throughout this process from the very beginning. I might drag you two into my next journey...again. haha

March 7th

Today marks seventeen years since you passed.
Today I celebrate you and will not be the last.
You were a survivor and a storyteller.
You were a giver and a father figure.
Gentle and kind.
Mindful and loved.
You crossed the bridge as cherry blossoms were blooming.
We played one of your favorite songs as you were leaving.
Here's to you on your anniversary.
The song you requested for the very last time to celebrate our memories.

"Do not stand at my grave and weep.

I am not there. I do not sleep.
I am a thousand winds that blow.
I am the diamond glints on snow.
I am the sunlight on ripened grain.
I am the gentle autumn rain.
When you awaken in the morning's hush, I am
the swift uplifting rush.
Of quiet birds in circled flight, I am the soft stars
that shine at night.
Do not stand at my grave and cry;
I am not there. I did not die."

A Thousand Winds by Mery E. Frye

IWD

Today is International Women's Day.
To me it's another ordinary day.
Another day to follow the examples of the women I respect.
The women who paved their way and helped others.

My favorite singer once said:
"Only the effort you put in will pay off."

Two of my favorite authors once said:
"If you can't change your fate, change your attitude," and "Make a difference about something other than yourself."

Two of my favorite humanitarians once said:

"Make bold choices and make mistakes. It's all those things that add up to the person you become," and "Everyone has a potential to give something back."

These are the women I acknowledge and celebrate for.
These are only a handful of women who had opened closed doors, and there are countless more.

Be influenced by good examples, not trends.
Be impressed by working smart and hard, not your statement.

Make your actions speak louder than your words.

3.11

Messages were flooding.
Images were running.
It was hard to process in my head to believe.
But it was easy to feel my heart racing to understand.

She was rumbling.
She was shaking.
She swept away many living things.
She sent them away from many loving souls.

Her waves of rage.
Her ways to engage.
Lives were carried by sea.
Memories were buried in sediment.

Scars she left behind.
Reminders to keep in mind.
Not to waste any given moment.
Lend a helping hand and know where you stand.

Where Do You Live?

Where do you live?
If you had asked me 30 years ago, I would have said Japan.
In a high-rise apartment at Marine Corps Air Station Iwakuni (MCAS Iwakuni).
Where I used to walk to the elementary school off base.
Where I used to walk to my mother's workplace after school every Saturday.
Where I used to walk to my father's part-time job when he was off duty.
Where my family and I used to go to Kintai Bridge and strolled around the park.
Where we used to go to Chikara Sushi or Sanzoku for dinner.

Where do you live?
If you had asked me 20 years ago, I would have said Japan.
In a triplex near MCAS Iwakuni.

Where I used to ride my bicycle to the train station and took a train to go to high school near the ocean.

Where my mother used to come home for lunch and we'd have lunch together during long breaks from school.

Where my mother, sister and I used to play badminton at Kikko Park, hiked up the mountain to get to Iwakuni Castle, and had ice cream to cool off.

Where we used to like going to Ganesh for authentic Indian food.

Where do you live?

If you had asked me 10 years ago, I would have said Japan.

In the same apartment in Iwakuni with my mother and sister.

Where I used to go to work driving my little Subaru.

Where I used to see my friends and meet their babies.

Where I used to grab drinks with colleagues after work.

Where I got my motorcycle license and went on bike rides with my colleagues.

Where my family and I used to go to Shiokaze Park and strolled down the beach.

Where do you live?
If you ask me now, I would say America.
In a duplex with a lakeview in Northern California.
Where I enjoy spending time reading and writing.
Where my partner and I go on food adventures on the weekends.
Where we look forward to going wine tasting at different vineyards.
Where we lived for nearly six months and soon will be moving again by the end of this spring.

Where do you live?
If you ask me 10 years from now, I might be living in a different state or somewhere overseas.
That's the beauty of life - you never know.

Now let me ask you.
Where do YOU live?

One Hour

If you could add one hour to your day,
What would you do with it?

Sleep in or work out?

Have breakfast with family,
Or have a cup of coffee and read a newspaper or articles on your cell phone?

Take an early bus/train to work,
Or drive and take a long way?

Catch up with colleagues,
Or knock off your tasks?

Take an extra hour of lunch break,
Or get off work an hour early?

Go straight home, kick back and relax,
Or treat yourself to happy hour?

Cook dinner or eat out?

Talk about your day with family during dinner,
Or scroll through social media while eating?

Watch your favorite show/movie after dinner,
Or read and enjoy the quietness?

Take a bubble bath,
Or take a longer shower than usual?

Meditate to unwind,
Or stretch before bed?

You can always add additional time by using your time wisely.
Time is gold.
Do not ever waste it.

Lakeview

As I run my pen on the paper,
I glanced outside and saw the water.

The sunlight hits the surface from above.
The skylight hits the room with warmth.
The wind applies glitter to the waves.
The blind could feel the sparkle in their hands.

Birds are chirping on the patio.
Ducks are chasing one another.
Absolute waterfowl paradise.
Chaotic at times but peaceful most times.

One lake in the backyard, but it offers different views everyday.

Choices

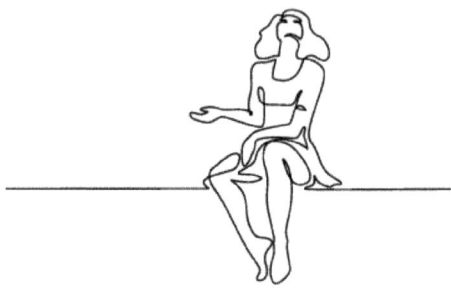

Being biracial was not my choice and challenging.
But being different was rewarding.
They were basic.
But I was exotic.

I've been told to return to my "country."
But the 6-year-old me refused to be ordinary.
They were still learning how to read.
I already knew how to write.

I've been told to change my hair color to blend in.
But my mother exchanged words to defend me.
She was a hardworking mother.
But she was definitely not a people pleaser.

I was an angry child in my early teens.
But I have never broken the law and
disappointed my family.
Peer pressure never bothered me.
I said no more than I said yes to avoid trouble.

Being bullied was my childhood.
Being accepted is my adulthood.
My choices brought me here.

We are what we choose to be.

Education

My grandmother once said, "People can take your belongings, but they can never take away your knowledge."

Education is key to life and success.
Education leads you to better opportunities.

People can be book smart and lack common sense.
People can be street smart and lack academic intelligence.

Education is not only in school.
Basic life skills.
Charities.
Creativity.
Cultural understanding.
Etiquette.

Mannerisms.
Netiquette.
Quality of life.
Respect.
Self improvement.
Time management.
And many more.
These can be taught at home.

In some countries, education is a necessity.
In some countries, education is a complexity.

For some people, education is costly.
For some people, education is forced.
For some people, education is an investment.
For some people, education is optional.

There is no time limit for education.
Challenge yourself and continue to learn.

Knowledge is power.

Air Show

Cloudless sky.
Endless horizon.
Bright sun on one side.
Shy moon on the other side.
Gentle breeze clears the air.

Familiar sounds of the aircrafts.
Different Air Show in a different country.
Reminds me of home.
But it gives me new excitement.

I grew up watching the Blue Impulse.
Today I got to watch the Blue Angels.
Flying freely on the blue canvas.
Leaving white contrails behind.

Must feel nice up there.
The more they flew higher, the more I wondered.
Seeing the world we can only imagine.
But sharing the fun we can all enjoy.

As they returned to the ground,
It was time to go home.
Strolled down to see their jets,
Hoping to see their performance again.

Good Luck

A pair of swallows.
Resting outside the window.
Winter has ended.
Spring has officially arrived.

Where there are swallows,
Many good luck will follow.
They are known as the symbol of new times
ahead and rebirth.

In some countries, they believe that swallows
are good luck and messengers of spring.
In some countries, they believe that good luck
will follow you along the way if you see a
swallow during your travels.

In some countries, they believe that swallows
bring prosperity and success wherever they go.

The swallow in the Bible is known as "the bird
of freedom."
Spiritually, swallows symbolize new beginning,
good luck, and hope.

As I watch the two swallows,
I think of these existing beliefs around the
world.
In this chaotic world we live in,
I am able to observe these birds ushering in the
new season peacefully.

As they fly off,
Life still goes on.
When they come back,
I hope they feel at home.

Here is my good luck wish to you.
Hoping that many of you will have better days
and brighter seasons ahead.

Halfway

I wanted to drop out after my sophomore year in university.
My mother suggested that I take a break instead.
Took a few years to return to school.
But I was able to graduate and receive my degree.

When I am unable to go home, I meet my family halfway.
Because they live too far away.
Wherever I may be in the world.
I find my way and hit the road.

Working on my eleventh poem.
Noticing that I am halfway done with this challenge.
I have never written a single poem in English in my life.

I could not imagine what this journey would be like.
But here I am halfway through.
Now I know that I can push my way through.

Reaching a goal is a long way.
Be proud if you made it halfway.
Even better if you can make one step.
For many, it is hard to make the first step.

Best Friend

It was early spring.
When cherry blossoms were starting to fall.
First day of elementary school.
In the same classroom.
That is when we met for the first time.

It was mid-summer.
When summer break was about to start.
My last day of school.
Before moving to America.
I kept your farewell letter.

It was early summer.
When my mom, my sister, and I returned to Japan.
I wrote you a letter.

You responded a few weeks later.
We became penpals.

It was early spring.
When spring break was about to start.
My last day of school.
Before moving back to the same city where we became friends.
We were classmates again a few weeks later.

It was early spring.
We started high school.
We went to different schools.
We kept in touch.
We made time to see each other.

It was early spring.
When I was in university, you were getting ready to study in America.
We promised we would write to each other.
And see each other when you are back in town.
We became penpals again.

It was early summer.
I moved to America.
Started going to a community college.
We called each other between classes.
It was nice to hear your voice when I had no friends at the time.

It was the middle of winter.
I returned to Japan to finish my degree.
You were getting ready to complete yours.
Facebook saved our time to communicate.
We no longer wrote letters, but we sent messages to each other.

It was early summer.
I started working in Japan.
You got a position and had to relocate to the Middle East.
We still visited each other or met halfway.
At this point, distance did not matter to us anymore.

Years have passed.
I live in America with my partner.
You live in Japan - happily married and are a proud mama.
Life became hectic, but we still talk on the phone and message each other when we have the chance.

Thirty-one years of friendship, and many more years to come.
I am truly proud to call you my best friend.

One Little Courage

One afternoon in the library.
Daydreaming more than studying.
You mustered up the courage to speak to me.
Not knowing we would become good friends.

We were both from the same country.
We spoke the same language.
We both had amber eyes and brown hair.
We had common understanding.

We met up between classes.
We hung out after class.
You helped me find a part-time job.
We saw each other almost every day - at school
and at work.

I remember your mother made me rice balls.
That made my day so much.
I remember being invited for dinner.
Being introduced to new cuisines yet felt like home.

After getting kicked out and having no place to go,
You and your parents offered a place to stay.
All of you told me that I could stay as long as I needed.
But the kindness I got from you and your parents was more than enough.

Five months later, I returned home with gratitude.
Four years later, I visited your hometown and reunited with you and your parents with excitement.
All the places we went, all the new foods I tried, I cherished every moment.
My heart was full with happiness on my flight back home.

Years later, I was fortunate to visit your parents for their promotion.
Few years later, I was fortunate again to visit your parents for their retirement.

Although we weren't able to see each other, your parents and your family kept me updated on your well-being.

Last summer, you came to America to visit your parents.
But I left for Japan to visit my family.
We were not able to see each other again.
But I really do hope to see you in the near future.

From the first "hello" to "see you again."
The little courage of yours kept our friendship for over a decade.
I sincerely wish our friendship will last our lifetime and be able to make many more memories with you and your amazing parents.

3.11 Reconstruction Volunteer

Two months after the disaster.
Took a week off from school.
Volunteered for the 3.11 Reconstruction Support.
Only three out of twelve hundred plus students
Volunteered from our university.
Approximately twenty people total have
attended from the city.

We were sent to Tagajo City in Miyagi
Prefecture.
Took us about fourteen hours to get there by bus.
The city itself lost nearly two hundred people by
the tsunami.
Half were residents outside of Tagajo City.

We were tasked to remove dirt.
From the houses and ditches.
It was still chilly.
But the season was shifting from spring to summer.

Constant aftershocks.
Dust flying in the air.
Surrounded by an unpleasant smell.
Work boots became muddy.
Work gloves became dirty.
Masks became dusty.
But we kept working.

Traces of water on exterior walls.
A lot higher than my height.
Dead and rotten fish were around the houses.
Nothing but mud in the houses.
Dolls, photos, a watch, etc.
Personal items were found as we continued to remove dirt from the ground.
Uncertain if the owners of these properties were still alive or not.
Our hearts sank.
But we kept working.

The neighboring residents were kind enough to offer us cold tea.
Felt very refreshing in our throats.

They thanked us for the heavy work.
We thanked them for sharing their stories while still recovering from the tragedy.

Many of them said,
"Emergency aid helps. Relief supplies help. But most importantly, people can only help people in a situation like this."

Interacting with people helps victims with their healing process.
They want volunteer members to spread the word and share awareness to others.

"When someone is in trouble, we can help each other."
This is what my mother said before I left for volunteering.
This was my very first volunteer work I have ever done.
I am glad I went, and I thank my mother for allowing me to go.
It was a short stay (for safety reasons), but I have learned a lot.

I was too young to remember the Great Hanshin Earthquake.
But I will remember the Great East Japan Earthquake.

One day in the near future, I would like to revisit Tagajo City and see how things have changed. I have added this wish to my bucket list.

Family Trip

Our very first family trip overseas.
It took us a while,
But we finally made it happen.
I still remember the excitement.
Of us planning and preparing for the trip.

Italy is one of my mother's favorite countries.
She still remembers some Italian.
She still remembers how things were like when she was actively traveling to Europe when she was young.
Sure enough, we were able to tour around Rome without Google Maps or any navigation apps.

Cute little hotel in Rome.
Cozy atmosphere.
Random calls from my mother's best friend who lives in a different city in Italy.
Complimentary breakfast to start our mornings.

Amazing museums after museums.

Detailed marble sculptures.
Breathtaking artworks.
Beautiful basilicas.

Strolling down the hill near the Colosseum.
Stopping by at a random local supermarket.
Amazed by different types of olive oils.
Sharing a table with strangers felt weird but it was a good experience.

All the walks didn't feel long at all.
Too many things to see in a short period of time.
The rain reminded us to slow down.
A rainbow peeked behind the Basilica of St. Mary of the Angels and Martyrs.

The view from Papal Basilica of St. Mary Major was absolutely spectacular.
Their white building looked even whiter under the blue sky.
Their two national flags were dancing in the wind.
As much as it was energetic in the outside,
It was peaceful and quiet inside.

Our adventure continued at night.
An evening bus tour to Vatican City.
As the sun went down,
the Vatican Museum began to glow.

When the city was beautifully lit,
We enjoyed our family dinner.

On our last day.
We strolled down to the Spanish Steps.
My sister had her portrait drawn by a street artist.
My mother enjoyed listening to a street opera singer.
I enjoyed capturing all these moments on my camera.
My sister and I had our first gelato outside of Japan.
Before we ended our day,
We made a wish at the Trevi Fountain.

It has been a while,
But I hope we can make another family trip to Europe again.

Dubai

My first trip to the Middle East.
My first flight with Emirates.
Departed in the evening, arrived in the morning.
Found my best friend at the arrival gate, holding a handmade "Welcome to Dubai" sign in her hands.

Her lovely condo was shared with other crew members.
High enough to enjoy the amazing view.
She made me a cup of tea to relax a bit.
Chatted a little before we left to grab a bite.

My first Camel Burger and *Luqaimat.
Dubai Museum to Desert Safari.
My first camel ride and Henna.
Sandboarding during sunset, and watching Arabian dance at night.

Morning visit to a temple nearby.
Downtown Dubai in the afternoon.

Enjoyed the afternoon tea at The Atmosphere of Burj Khalifa.
Magnificent view of Burj Al Arab in the distance during dusk.
Beautiful fountain show in the evening.
Luckily, we got to see the Burj Khalifa fireworks for the Dubai Expo 2020 win.
Absolutely memorable.

Wherever I go, I love Old Village/Town/City visits.
Crossing the Dubai Creek on an *Abra was my favorite.
Historic districts, traditional markets, and day-to-day life still exist.
Wandering around the maze-like streets was my favorite, too.

Fun times always fly.
Like a blink of an eye.
Woke up to a cup of freshly made Arabic coffee.
This little surprise from a cabin crew made my trip complete.

*Luqaimat - The Middle East style doughnut balls.
*Abra - Traditional boat made of wood. It means "to cross" in Arabic.

Food Adventures

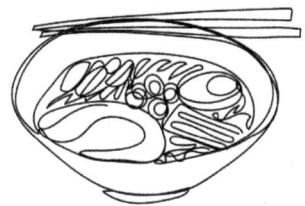

My response was "no" for a good two months.
My colleague was stubborn enough to invite me out for an International Food Festival.
We invited one of his colleagues and went to the festival.
It was an awfully hot summer day in *DMV.

The festival was crowded.
Which was expected.
We strolled through the vendors.
We ended up staying there for hours.

We tried Okonomiyaki, Tamales, and a few more.
We went to *CVS for water - the waters sold at the vendors were EXPENSIVE.
We watched dances and shows from different country groups which we enjoyed.

Later on in the evening,

We went bar hopping.
Got lost to find my colleague's car.
Saw him run for the first time when we found his vehicle.

It was supposed to be a few hours or maybe a half day outing.
Turned out to be an all day food adventure.
We ate a lot, we drank enough.

Since then, our food adventures have become our monthly event.
We tried:
- Different types of Burgers
- Different types of Fried Chickens
- Different types of Ramen Noodles
- Japanese Souffle Pancakes
- Lots of Korean food (Bingsu, Korean BBQ, Korean Corn Dogs, etc.)
- Rolled Ice Cream
- Shawarmas
- Variety of foods from the Dutch Market
And many more.

Now we live away from each other,
But our food adventures will resume as soon as we get together.

*CVS - Consumers Value Stores
*DMV - Washington D.C., Maryland, and Virginia

Daydreamer

I get lost in daydreams.
For some, it's a distraction from the present.
To me, it's a vacation time for my busy mind.

I get lost in daydreams.
I may appear quiet and reserved.
Actually, I have the loudest mind and am observant.

I get lost in daydreams.
Maybe because I do not dream a lot when I am sleeping.
I dream a lot when I am awake.

I get lost in daydreams.
What do I dream about?
Everything and anything.

What Made You Smile?

What made you smile lately?

I was at a birthday party last weekend.
I saw my partner's one year old nephew.
Marching his way towards his mother.
Bumped his little head on the bottom of a table,
Unbothered and kept on going.
Thought he might cry as he touched his head,
But acted as if nothing happened.
Made me realize that he is growing and I smiled.

A couple of weeks ago, I was sitting by the window.
In the corner of my eye, I saw a duck chasing another duck.
I looked outside of the window and saw them running the opposite direction.

Shaking their behinds like Corgis and made me chuckle.

These events do not seem to be special at all.
Though laughter can be found in daily life in little moments.
No need to scroll through social media.
No need to rely on entertainment shows.

Sit back and observe.
Pay attention and listen.
You might see something that will make you smile.
You might hear something that will make you chuckle.

What made you smile today?

Where Would You Go?

If you could travel anywhere tomorrow,
Where would you go?

I would go to Japan to visit my family.
Maybe visit my friends too.
Cherry blossoms are in full bloom now.
Perfect time to enjoy the spring.

Or I would go to Spain to visit their old towns.
Spectacular cathedrals and palaces.
Monuments and walls.
Learn their rich history through their people.

Or I would go to Monaco to enjoy the Grand Prix.
Visit the Oceanographic Museum by the ocean.
Soak up the sun at the beaches.
Admire the yachts passing by.

Or I would go to Tahiti just to kick back and relax.

Feel the warm sand and water.
Listen to the waves.
Try their street foods.
Swim with tropical fish.

So many places I would like to travel.

Where would you go?

Simplest Pleasure

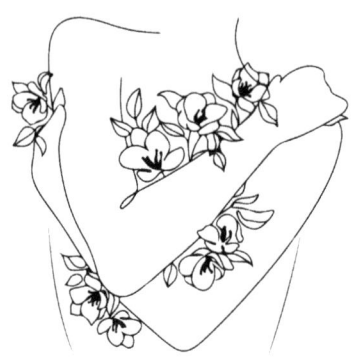

Give me a cup of coffee and I will be content.
Cappuccino in the morning.
Café Latte during coffee break.
Mocha when I want something chocolatey but stronger than hot cocoa.

Give me a book and you will make my day.
Rom-Com when I am feeling down.
Suspense when I am feeling stressed.
Historical when I feel like learning.
Let me borrow your favorite book so I can get to know you better.

Kidnap me on a trip and I will be your lifelong friend.
Road trip to grab food.

Meet halfway and get lost in a city we have never been to.
Book a flight at the last minute and travel overseas.

Show me a positive attitude and you will have my attention.
Talk about something I do not know.
Tell me stories of your own.
Educate me.

I pick and choose.
But most times I am easy to please.
I get excited with the simplest things.
That is also because I am grateful for the smallest things.

Rejection is Redirection

I have been rejected by classmates,
Because I was "different."
I have been rejected by strangers,
Because I was a "foreigner."
I have been rejected for jobs,
Because I did not meet their "expectations."
And many can relate.

I was redirected to meet new friends,
Because others genuinely liked me for who I am.
I was redirected to new places,
Because there are many other places where you are welcomed.
I was redirected to new opportunities,
Because others saw potential in me.
And so do other people.

Take rejection as an opportunity.
Opportunity to be redirected to a better place.

Hero

Sailor Jupiter was my childhood hero.
Tough but thoughtful.
Strong and protective.
I wanted to become a Sailor Soldier rather than a Disney Princess.

*Namie Amuro was, and still is, my hero since I was a tween.
Modest but powerful.
Strong-willed and beautiful – inside and out.
Although she has been retired from the music biz,
I still listen to her music often.

My mother has been my hero and always will be.
Strong and attentive single mother of two daughters.
A big sister I never had.

She is my human diary.
I want to be like her when I grow up.

It is true that real heroes don't wear capes.

"I'll be your hero just for you.
I'll be by your side no matter what.
I'll be your hero.
And you are my hero."

Hero by Namie Amuro

*Namie Amuro – Retired Japanese singer.

Sister

She likes to draw.
She likes to read.
She likes to watch anime.
She likes to go to art and music events.

She is the funny one.
She is the peacemaker.
She is the quiet one in public.
She is the chatty one at home.

We went to school together.
We pranked mom together.
We hung out together more than we did with our friends.
Although there were times we did not talk.

We used to argue a lot.
We used to fight a lot.
I used to be rough on her.
I made her cry more than enough.

She is my partner in crime.
She is my other half.
She is a portion of my life.
Proud to call her my sister.

New Beginning Awaits

This is my last poem.
For #TheWriteAngle Writing Challenge.
It was hard, but also fun.
Few hours a day for twenty-one days.
I jotted down my thoughts on my notebook.

I focused on good memories to share.
So much to select from.
I might try another challenge.
So I can continue to share more of my stories and thoughts.

Once my book is released,
My mother will be the first person to receive a copy.
It could be a belated Mother's Day gift,
Or an early birthday gift.

Since I moved to America,
I did nothing but worry her.
I broke up with my ex-fiancé.

I was broke.
I was depressed.
I was not in a good place for about a handful of years.
I could have dropped everything and returned home.
But I did not want to give up.

After attempting to focus on good things,
I found a mentor who I respect very much.
I was fortunate to work with like-minded colleagues.
I found a few good friends.
I found a partner who I can trust and feel safe to be with - financially, mentally, and physically.
And lastly, I wanted to do something that I have been wanting to do for a long time.

I can confidently say to her,
That I am doing okay.

Although I am fully aware that my poems are not perfect,
This writing process was very special to me.
This chapter of my story ends.
But I hope I can deliver more stories to my readers in much better condition in the near future.

XOXO,
Nicole

Printed in the USA
CPSIA information can be obtained
at www.ICGtesting.com
LVHW012310300524
781885LV00007B/256